So great a God

BY

Mary Cundy

D1321509

Made in Great Britain
Published by BMMF International (UK)
186 Kennington Park Road, London SE11 4BT

ISBN 0 900165 08 1

Printed in Great Britain by
Errey's Printers Ltd., Streatfield Road, Heathfield,
East Sussex

GLOSSARY

Main Characters

Santa Kumari   *A Nepali widow woman*

Saraswati   *Santa Kumari's sister*

Sheti   *Santa Kumari's daughter*

Maya   *Santa Kumari's sister-in-law*

Bhimsen   *Santa Kumari's son*

Putali   *Bhimsen's wife*

Chandri   *Santa Kumari's married daughter*

Man Bahadur   *Chandri's husband*

Juthe   *Maya's son*

Mukhia Prem Lal   *Headman of Chisopani*

Jyote   *Brahmin girl, social worker trainee at the Hospital*

Lal Bahadur   *Hospital trainee and leprosy patient*

Pator Dhanraj   *Pastor of church in Baltachaur*

PREFACE TO THE FIRST EDITION

THE question is often asked how the Gospel can spread in a land like Nepal, where open-air preaching, or evangelistic meetings are not officially allowed, and where there are severe penalties for changing your religion.

I hope that this story will give some answers to that question. All the events recorded are true and happened in Nepal, but in the lives of many different people and not in the sequence found here. I have merely put them together to make a story which I hope will give an idea of what it means to be a Christian in Nepal.

I pray that this book may stimulate prayer for the gallant people of that lovely land of Nepal and the Church there.

I would thank Miss H. Steele for her help and advice and Mrs. M. Holmwood and Miss C. Root for their assistance with typing.

MARY CUNDY 1974

PREFACE TO THE THIRD EDITION

SINCE the first edition of this book in 1974, it has been wonderful to see, in answer to the prayers of many people around the world, the growth of the Church in Nepal.

Since to change your religion can still bring imprisonment, persecution and other hardships, the question is often asked how the Gospel has reached so many.

It was to give some answer to that question that I first wrote this book, and I am glad that the story still has relevance to the growth of the Church today. All the happenings in this book are based on people and events that actually took place in Nepal.

I pray that this third edition may continue to stimulate prayer for the gallant people of the lovely land of the Gurkhas and for the Church there.

Machhapuchare (Fishtail Mountain) from Pokhara

SO GREAT A GOD

CHAPTER ONE

DAWN was breaking over the eastern mountains, edging them with silver light, but in the room where Santa Kumari lay alone on her mat, half sleeping, half waking, it was still dark. Somewhere in the fields below the house a deer barked, a sudden, sharp sound that set the monkeys chattering in a nearby tree.

Roused by the tumult, the woman sat up and ran a hand through her hair with a weary gesture. Another day. What would it bring? Fresh calamity? More trouble? Or might it bring a word from Sheti? She brightened at the thought of possible news from her daughter. Rising to her feet she smoothed down her crumpled sari and tightened her *patuka* —the brightly coloured cloth that swathed her waist. Then rolling up her rice-straw mat she thrust it behind the rafters and went outside.

By now the light had strengthened, spreading swiftly down the mountain slopes. Already it was giving colour to the hillside which fell away steeply below her house, terraced field upon terraced field. Mist lay thickly in the valley where soon the villagers would be working in their fields; it hid every gorge and ravine, and wreaths of it softened the contours of thrusting peaks. And from where she stood on the tiny verandah Santa Kumari could see, away to the south, the blue hills which separated her country from India.

Her thoughts, however, were not on the landscape; they were with her daughter Sheti. Had she done right to let the girl go to the hospital at Baltichaur? It was so far away over the mountains—so unknown. But what else could she have done? It would have been madness to keep her in the village. Some day, the dreadful disease would show itself on her face and her mother knew what that would mean. Had she not watched her own brother die, shunned and neglected to the end by the villagers because of this curse? And now her sister Saraswati had been hounded from the village, made to live alone in a shack in the jungle. Poor Saraswati! She hadn't realised what the trouble was until her face had begun to swell. Even then she had managed to keep her condition hidden, covering her face with her shawl, until one morning, as she lifted her waterpot into the basket slung on her back, her shawl had slipped . . .

"Did you see Saraswati's face? Hasn't she got leprosy?"

It had been only a whisper but Saraswati had heard it and it had been enough to send the truth all round the district. Almost at once the village elders had been there to tell her she must get out. She had refused to move at first and finally they had stoned her out of the village. They thought they were justified in what they were doing, thought Santa Kumari. Everybody knows how infectious leprosy is. *But this must not happen to Sheti.*

Santa Kumari shivered as she turned to the task of cleaning the verandah. Today it must be done extra well for this was Divali, Festival of Lights, when everybody honoured the goddess Lakshmi. People said that if your house pleased the goddess she would visit you and bring good luck. And wasn't Lakshmi the goddess of Wealth? A visit from her could mean so much. So Santa took special care as she smoothed the wet mud over the floor. Later she would get the small oil wicks ready to set around the verandah at dusk. She would buy more this year. She would set the verandah ablaze with light so that the goddess should not miss her way.

She paused as she reached for the red ochre to daub on the front step and looked up at the high Himalayan mountains that rose majestically behind her house, beyond her own mountain range. The eternal snows! The dwelling place of the gods, or so men said. Perhaps if she had made a pilgrimage up there she could have appeased those gods who surely must be angered with her family, so much trouble had they sent. But what was the use of thinking in this way; she could never have afforded such a trip. And who had ever returned from a pilgrimage having found what he went to seek? But what about Sheti? Would she find that there really is a god in Baltichaur who heals leprosy?

By evening there was still no news from Sheti. Santa sighed as she trimmed the oil lamps set around the verandah and listened to the sound of singing coming from the village below. There would be a great deal of drinking going on, she knew; there always was at festival time. She wondered if her nephew Juthe was there among the drinkers. It was quite likely, his mother being away. She had gone with Sheti to Baltichaur. Santa looked up as her son Bhimsen came on to the verandah.

"*Namasthe!* Greetings to you, Mother. Do you know where Jhute is?" he asked.

"In the village, I expect," replied his mother. "And probably drinking hard. I'm sorry his mother is away."

Bhimsen turned in surprise. "Where has she gone?"

"She's gone to Baltichaur and taken Sheti with her."

"When is she likely to be back?"

"I don't know. I wish they were here, but I suppose they must be staying until after Divali."

Bhimsen grinned. "Well, no doubt they are having a good time. There is plenty going on in Baltichaur these days."

"Maya, poor thing, won't have much to spend having had so much expense with her husband's funeral. I do hope Juthe doesn't get involved with that gambling group in the village."

"Don't worry, Mother. I'll keep an eye on him!"

9

"Yes, see that you do. And don't you go drinking too much either, wasting all our money. We are in debt deeply enough with the Brahmins without you and Juthe making it worse. Don't stay there all night. I think there's a storm coming."

"Yes, it certainly looks black toward Annapurna. I expect you have heard that they have sacrificed old Ratan's black goat? They had a special *puja* this morning and there is a feast in the village tonight. The headman invited me." His mother looked pleased.

"Is Juthe going as well?"

"Oh, I expect so. Did you hear that they had another reason for killing the black goat besides the usual Divali sacrifice? It was to prevent any more leprosy coming to the village." Bhimsen laughed. "They thought if they killed such a big black goat there might be enough blood to keep the gods happy for a time!"

"Don't mock, Bhimsen," said his mother unhappily. "I know that since you have been to school you have been inclined to throw over the old customs. But the gods are to be feared."

"Oh, I know, Mother. Well, I'm off to join Juthe."

Santa finished trimming the lamps and went into the house. How lonely it was without Sheti, and how she missed Maya's evening visits. Sounds of singing came up from the village but she had no inclination to go down and watch or to join the gambling and feasting. She would make herself some millet bread, curry the remains of the chicken and then go to bed. She was very tired for she had had a busy day, cleaning and cooking. Then there had been the long walk up to the temple at the top of the hill. It had exhausted her, but with all that had happened to her family she had felt she must make an effort and go. You never knew what might happen if you were to offend the gods.

She ate her meal, washed the cup and plate and then spreading her rice-straw mat she curled up to sleep. But she did not go to sleep. Instead she lay looking at the familiar objects in her home, visible because of the tiny lamps still burning outside—two or three cooking pots standing upside down by the fireplace, a bucket and a kettle, a bundle of wood ready chopped. Two brass plates stood against the wall, winking where the light caught their polished surface. The blade of her sharp knife gleamed among the rafters where she had pushed it along with her precious comb, her flint and a bit of broken mirror.

No, there was not much in her home, but she loved it. Her thoughts went back to the time when her husband had built it from stones found on the hillside. His friends had helped him build the walls but her task had been to plaster them inside and out with mud and cowdung. Maya had helped her. They had made it a two-storeyed house, and how proud her husband had been to be able to do so. They had had a good year with the crops and had sold some of the goats in order to do it but it had been wonderful to have a room upstairs in which to store grain when the lower mud-floor was damp with the rains. Yes, thought Santa, things had been good in the old days. But now . . . ?

She must have fallen asleep at last for it was a sound of knocking that startled her into wakefulness. She did not know what time it was, only that it was deep night and the lamps on the verandah had burned out. Pulling her sari tightly around her, she opened the door and the two lads almost fell on top of her.

"Bhimsen! Juthe! What is the matter? What a storm! You are soaking wet. One of you get me a light." But they simply sank in a heap on the floor and she had to light the lamp herself. There was a strong smell of liquor as she bent over them to shake them.

"What has happened?" she cried. "Why have you not gone home?"

"It's Saraswati;" Bhimsen eventually managed to get it out though his speech was slurred.

"What about Saraswati?"

"She's gone!"

11

"Gone? What do you mean?"

Bhimsen groaned. "Her hut's not there. She's gone."

"How do you know?"

"Daju said there is no sign of the hut."

"Well, we'd better go and see if we can help her."

"No use," he protested. "Can't go in this storm."

"Oh, you are useless," cried Santa despairingly. "I'll have to go on my own."

"No use" repeated Bhimsen thickly and turned on his side. Juthe was already sunk in a drunken sleep.

Santa went to the door and looked out. The storm was still raging and it was pitch dark. She realised that she could not possibly go out just then. Would the rain never cease? Would dawn never come? If only the two lads were not so drunk. It was no use looking for help from them for some time.

As dawn broke, she went out alone into the rain, down the mud path, slipping, sliding along the hillside until she came to the point above where the shack had been. She looked down and exclaimed in horror. A landslide had carried everything before it. Trees had been blown down and there was no sign of the hut or its occupant.

Slowly she began the climb down, her sari catching in the scrub. The leeches bit viciously and she could feel the blood running down her legs. Arriving at the place where the hut had been she found it difficult to see further down the hill. She would have to go on. She began to descend slowly on the slippery clay where once the path had been, leading down to the stream several hundred feet below. She stumbled on, calling her sister's name as she went, but all she heard was the echo of her own voice in reply. "Oh, where is she?" Santa cried, staggering on down, and still further down, until at last she saw what appeared to be a pile of leaves and bamboo. What was that beside it? She slid down the last few feet.

The sight that met her eyes caused her to hold her breath

12

in horror. Saraswati lay in a heap, her sari torn and blood-stained. She crawled nearer and saw that her head was injured; blood had oozed from a wound on her temple. She took the hand lying limply on the grass and again called Saraswati by name. But there was no response.

"Oh, she's dead!" she wailed, and began to sob.

She sat for a while in the rain, weeping over the dead woman, then the horror of the situation swept over her. She would have to go to the village and get someone to help her carry Saraswati's body up the hill. And who would touch one who had leprosy?

A well in Pokhara

CHAPTER TWO

THE two women walked slowly up the hill in the gathering dusk.

"I think we shall get to Samrai before dark," said Maya cheerfully.

"I hope so, because then we can stay with Jagat. Not much further now, just over the top and along the ridge and we shall be in the village. Let's rest on this *chautara* and put our baskets down. Mine seems to be so heavy and is rubbing on my back."

Sheti slipped the bands slowly off her head and shoulders and let her basket down gently on to the stone platform built specially for the resting of weary travellers. "Old Oman Singh built this chautara, didn't he, Aunt Maya? Did he do it to gain merit?"

"I suppose so—and to appease the gods. He had a bad cough for years and the priest up at Bhograti said it was an evil spirit. The old man paid an awful lot of money out for cocks and goats for sacrifice and built this resting place. But it was no use, he died of his cough."

Sheti nodded. "He had a lot of trouble, didn't he? But no more than we have had. We've had more than our share, haven't we?"

"We have indeed," replied Maya. "It was awful to see my Jarhu suffer so much before he died, and so hard to keep him hidden all the time so that people wouldn't know he had leprosy. I would do anything to see that you don't suffer in the same way, Sheti."

'It was good of you to come with me, Aunt Maya. I wonder if they really can do anything for us at Baltichaur? I liked the two young men who came from there. Though I couldn't understand all they said, somehow their words gave me hope."

"Come, it will be dark if we don't go now. Mind you keep your sari well around you, Sheti. We don't want people to get suspicious. Remember, we are going to Baltichaur about Jarhu's pension. We must not let Jagat know we are going to the new Hospital."

They pushed on over the hill and walked along the ridge. It was a lovely evening. Over the ranges, they could see the Himalayas their towering white peaks turning pink in the evening sunset, the Fish Tail Annapurna range and Dhaulagiri darkly outlined against the northern sky. They were both occupied with their own thoughts as they trudged along. Maya was remembering again her husband's long illness, the terror of trying to keep the villagers from knowing he had leprosy. She looked at Sheti, striding along beside her. Perhaps she had not that disease at all! How wonderful it would be if that were so; but Maya hadn't much hope.

Sheti, too, was thinking about her trouble. What was going to happen to her? What would it be like at the Hospital? She had heard that these foreigners did awful things to people. Had she really got leprosy? She shuddered at the thought of all that could happen to her—the spreading of the marks on her face, the possible loss of her fingers and toes. How ghastly and frightening it all was. Well, maybe it wasn't leprosy at all but just something similar, some skin trouble for which she could get medicine. Oh, if that were so, she would do the biggest *puja* ever and give all her life to the service of the gods.

It was Maya who broke the silence. "Here we are and just in time. There is Jagat on the verandah lighting his oil lamps. *Namastai*, Jagat!"

16

The man, a distant relative of theirs, turned and peered at them. *"Namastai!* Who is it? Oh, it's you Maya, and is it Sheti with you? Sit down and I'll call Bishnu." He turned back to the door and called his wife.

Bishnu came out at once and greeted them. *"Namastai!* Where have you come from and where are you going?"

"We have come from Chisopani and are on our way to Baltichaur."

"Well! How is everybody in Chisopani? Come in and I'll get you a meal."

Maya and Sheti followed her. "We have rice here," said Maya, dropping her basket to the floor. "I'll give it to you."

While Bishnu cooked the rice and made a curry of wild vegetables over a wood fire in the centre of the mud floor, the women sat around and talked.

"What happened to Jharu, Maya?" asked Bishnu presently, giving the rice a stir and testing it between finger and thumb. "Did you take his body to the Kali river?"

"Yes, and a lot of expense it was. I had to sell several goats. But it was the right thing to do."

Bishnu sighed. "Yes, it is certainly our duty to see that they are cared for, not only in this world but in the next. Do you expect to get a pension? You should, after all his service in the army."

Maya nodded. "At least I can go and enquire."

"They say things have altered a lot in Baltichaur since the coming of the aeroplanes," said Bishnu. "And I have heard there are foreigners there too. They have started a Hospital. It sounds all right. Thom Bahadur got mangled by a bear about two months ago and had a badly torn face. Prem went to see him and stopped the bleeding with the spider-web mixture. His face improved but not his arm which the bear had mangled. Prem put a casing of cowdung on that and after some days Thom was in such agony that he asked to be taken to Baltichaur. We thought that would be the last we should see of him but he has come back this week and seems to be healed. He has such tales to tell, too!"

17

"What sort of tales?"

"Oh, such as being made to sleep in a bed! He wasn't allowed to sleep on the ground. His wife who went with him had to do the cooking in another place and wasn't allowed to put her cooking pots under the bed! Also he was told not to spit! How do they expect you to get your throat cleared if you don't spit, I don't know!"

"Could he understand what the foreigners said?"

"Oh, yes. Thom says they speak our language. That surprised him for when our folk go with the army to another country, they often do not seem to understand the language. You may see some of these white people when you are in Baltichaur."

"Maybe we shall," said Maya.

Next morning, Sheti and Maya rose early, rolled up their mats and bade farewell to Bishnu who alone was awake to see them off. A long walk lay ahead of them, and a steady one if they were to reach the Hospital by noon. They did not talk much as they made their way down the steep path. They went carefully for the morning dew had made the red earth slippery and treacherous. Nor were they aware of the magnificent scenery around them, the thrusting hills, ridge lifting behind ridge, with far away above and behind them the eternal snows, flushed where the rising sun touched them.

Maya and Sheti had never travelled far from Chisopani. Some of their relatives had gone away to join the Ghurkha forces and brought back stories of far away places outside Nepal but the women had not been affected much. The daily routine of life had gone on—the carrying of water and collecting of fodder for goats and buffaloes, the tending of fields and the appeasing of the gods. It was a new thing for them to be going as far as Baltichaur.

The sun had fully risen by the time they reached the valley and the wind had whisked the last floating scarf of mist away. They crossed the shallow stream then began the climb up to the last pass, the opening in the mountains from where they would see the Hospital. They made a striking picture as they climbed with the steady gait of the hill peasant, tiny figures in a gigantic landscape, but very colourful. Maya wore her best, long-sleeved red velvet blouse and her waist bound with the yellow cloth that served to keep her flowered black skirt in place. A folded square of brightly coloured print was tied over her neatly plaited hair and a triangular piece of the same material hung from her left shoulder, covering back and chest and falling almost to the knees. Sheti wore a bright blue sari and her *patuka* also was a vivid yellow. Both women carried the conical baskets on their backs, suspended by a knotted rope slung from their foreheads.

They were beginning to feel weary by the time they reached the pass and began to descend again.

"Not much further now, Aunt Maya," said Sheti excitedly. "Look! Isn't that the hospital on top of the other hill?"

Maya followed the direction of Sheti's pointing finger and saw a long, low brick building nestling against the farther hillside and surrounded by narrow terraced fields of grain. They stared at it in awe. They didn't need to be told that every brick in that (to them) vast building, all the stonework and all that might be found inside the building, had been carried up from the valley on the backs of local people.

I'm feeling scared," said Sheti. "I wonder what will happen to us. Aren't you scared, Aunt Maya?"

"No, but I wish we had a man with us. They may not listen to us women."

"Thom said one of the doctors is a woman. Perhaps we shall see her."

"Really? A woman doctor? And here are we who cannot even read."

"Have you seen many white people, Aunt Maya?"

"No, not many, and with their funny clothing I find it difficult sometimes to know which are men and which are women. But here we are at Putlikhat. Let's have our meal here. *Namastai!*"

Her greeting was for a woman who had come to the door

of a house as they approached. *"Namastai.* Where have you come from and where are you going?" she asked, eyeing them curiously.

We have come from Chisopani and are going to Baltichaur."

"Why are you going to Baltichaur?"

"My husband died recently and we are going to see about his pension," said Maya. "We have rice with us; could you cook it for us?"

"Of course," said the woman, taking the bundle. She went inside and was there for some time while the two women sat on the verandah. "Was your husband ill for long?" she asked, returning and standing in the doorway.

"No, he died suddenly."

"May the gods be merciful to you! Have you seen the new Hospital? There are white people there. One of them was down here last week with the Brahmin girl who helps at the Hospital. They had a meal here and I noticed that they shut their eyes before they ate their food. They said they were praying for God's blessing on my house and thanking Him for their food."

"It's strange you should mention that. Thom Bahadur from our village has been in the Hospital and he said they are called the 'shut-eye party'! But he also said that people are afraid of them because when they shut their eyes and speak to God, they really do seem to talk to a spirit."

"Yes, the people who live around here are not afraid now to go across that hillside above us. They never used to go that way because of the spirits of dead animals thrown there that haunted it. But it seems they are not there now because the Spirit that is with the folk at the Hospital is more powerful than the spirits of dead animals. That Spirit must be very powerful otherwise they would never have built on haunted land nor taken Devi Prasad's house in the bazaar which has been empty for years because of the evil spirit there. The two Hospital women who came the other day left a booklet

—now where is it? You might like it. I don't want it; my husband was angry when he saw it."

"We don't read," said Maya, "But my nephew Bhimsen has been learning so he might like it."

"Here it is, and here is your meal ready."

"We will eat it and be getting on."

They ate their rice, then started up the last, long hill to the hospital. At the bazaar in Baltichaur town they were directed to the path that would lead them to the Hospital. They had arrived at last.

Village houses

CHAPTER THREE

SANTA Kumari stumbled blindly back up the hillside to the path at the top. Here she turned right and ran as quickly as she could to the centre of the village where the headman's house stood.

"Where is Mukhia Premlal?" she gasped.

The headman's family gathered around her. "What's the matter?" they asked.

"It's Saraswati. She was swept down the hill by the storm. She is dead and I want help to get her body up the hill."

"You will get no help from Premlal; he has gone away. And it's no use asking us; you know we can't touch her. You'd better get your own family to help you."

"Maya and Sheti are away. I'll have to send word to my daughter Chandri and her husband, but Man Bahadur is too weak to do much."

"What about Bhimsen and Juthe?"

"They are drunk and in no fit state to know what they are doing."

"Well, you won't get any help from us. Your family have already brought enough trouble on the village. You know that leprosy is a curse from the gods so how can we touch Saraswati whom the gods have cursed? What do you think would happen to us if we did? We don't want their wrath to fall on us and our families."

"Yes, I know that. But I can't leave her there. Jackals may come."

"Well, go and get her yourself if the boys won't help."

Seeing that it was useless to talk to the villagers, Santa turned back home. The two boys were still lying on the floor. She shook them impatiently. "Bhimsen! Juthe! Wake up! Wake up!"

"Oh dear! Bhimsen groaned. "What's the matter? Oh, my head; how it aches!"

"Do come, Bhimsen. It's Saraswati. She's dead. Her hut was washed down the hill and she was killed."

"Dead, Mother? She can't be!"

"I tell you, she is. I saw her. When the hut was swept away, she went with it. Oh, it is too awful. She *is* dead, I tell you. Come now and help me get her body up from the jungle."

"No, I'm not going to touch her!"

Santa wrung her hands despairingly. "We can't leave her there, and no one in the village will help me."

"Mother, you are not to touch her".

"I've already touched her, and I'll have to touch her again, I must go and get her."

She left them and returned to the path that led to the spot where Saraswati's body lay. The rain had stopped and she found a group of villagers, mostly women, standing looking down the hillside.

"Oh, here she is, Santa Kumari, what are you going to do?" asked one.

"She is your sister. You will have to go down and get the body," said another.

Santa said: "Will none of you help me?"

They shook their heads. "How can we run such a risk? We have our own families to think of."

"But I can't do it alone," Santa pleaded.

"You'll have to do it. We're sorry but we can't touch her."

Santa climbed slowly down to where her sister's body lay. Gathering leafy branches, she covered her back with them

24

and then pulled the dead woman on to her shoulders and began to crawl up the hill, supporting the body by a rope sling, the band of which she adjusted to her forehead to take the weight. The folk at the top shrank away as she appeared over the brow of the hill. She struggled along until she came to the courtyard of her own house. Here, Bhimsen and Juthe were standing looking rather shamefaced. Santa laid her burden on the ground.

"Bhimsen, here are ten rupees. Go and buy some white cloth."

"Cloth, Mother?" cried Bhimsen. "What for?"

"Oh, don't be so stupid! To wrap the body in, of course."

"But who is going to bury her? We can't carry her."

"It looks as if you will have to," said Santa wearily. "But here comes Prem Lal. *Namastai,* ji." Her greeting was for the headman who had appeared at the door.

"Namastai, Santa Kumari. So Saraswati was swept down the hillside last night. I hear she is dead."

"She is dead indeed, and who will help me with the body?"

"Well, Bhimsen won't want to touch it, that's certain. And how's Juthe? Still getting over last night's drinking? I will tell the *Sarkis* (low caste) they are to assist you."

"Oh, you will, will you? Well, we won't do it", said a voice from the small group of people who had gathered.

"You must," was the headman's curt command.

"Why should we do it when others won't" they muttered.

"How much do you want? Ten rupees each?"

Santa gave a cry. "Where am I going to get ten rupees each for them?" she asked.

"We won't do it for ten, that's certain."

The headman argued on with the leader of the *Sarkis* but it was no use. After a while he and the crowd went away, leaving Santa with the body.

When Bhimsen returned with the white cloth, she wrapped the body in it. "You had better go and tell your sister

Chandri, and Man Bahadur, to come and tell me what I should do," she said.

It was late afternoon when Bhimsen, having walked three hours to Man Bahadur's house, returned with his sister and her husband. Santa Kumari, weeping, told them what had happened.

"I'll go to the headman's house and see what can be done," said Man Bahadur. When he came back some time later he said: *"Sarkis* Bhim Lal and Hem Lal will take the body for cremation by the river but they want thirty rupees each."

"Thirty rupees each! Where am I to get sixty rupees?" cried Santa Kumari.

"You will have to sell your big white goat, that's the only way. We can't leave her here and the village is already angry with us for bringing this disgrace on them. The men are on their way now. Where are Bhimsen and Juthe? They will have to come with me to the river."

Santa looked startled. "You can't go now. The roads will be far too slippery and you won't be back before nightfall."

"No, we must go now. We can't put the body inside anywhere. Here come the lads. We will be going at once. You arrange to sell the goat."

The two low caste men tied the clothbound body to a long pole they had brought with them and hoisted it on to their shoulders. Man Bahadur, Bhimsen and Juthe walked behind. Santa Kumari and Chandri watched them going down the path to the river until they were out of sight. "What have we done to incur the wrath of the gods that we have to bear so much?" said Chandri as they turned back sadly into the house.

CHAPTER FOUR

THE hospital was much bigger seen at close quarters than it had appeared from the other hill. "I have never seen anything like it!" exclaimed Maya. "I wonder what we should do now?"

"I don't know. Let's sit here on the hillside and watch for a while. Look, there is someone being carried in a basket. Let us see what they do. Oh, they don't know where to go either; they are asking. He must be a very important man, he has so many people with him."

"If they have people like this, maybe they won't look at us," said Maya nervously. "Let's follow them in and see what happens."

They found themselves in a large, cement-walled room with several doors opening from it. At one side, people were crowding round a man who sat in a box-like compartment, writing in a book. There were benches in the centre which seemed to be occupied mainly by male patients. Some people were lying on improvised stretchers on which they had been carried from distant villages, others were sitting on the coconut matting that covered the floor.

Maya and Sheti felt very much alone and bewildered as they stood in the doorway and looked around them. Sheti clutched Maya and said: "What should we do, Aunt Maya? What a crowd!"

"*Namastai!*" The two women looked up at the girl who

27

greeted them. She was dressed in a dark blue sari over a pale blue blouse and though she smiled at them in a warm and friendly manner she looked alert and efficient. "Where are you from?" she asked as they returned her greeting. "Have you come to see the doctor? Is this your first visit?"

"Yes, we are from Chisopani."

"Have you got your ticket?"

"Tickets?"

"Yes, your ticket which you must have before you can see the doctor. It will have your number on. Go and queue at the desk over there and get your name written."

"You go, Aunt Maya," said Sheti nervously.

The girl smiled. "Is she the patient?"

"No, I am the patient."

"Then it is your name we need. Just a minute and I will come with you and help you."

Sheti had her name written and then went and sat down to wait until it was time to go to the doctor. "It was a good thing that girl helped us, wasn't it, Aunt Maya? We might have been sitting here all day. I was surprised she was so friendly, weren't you? I'm sure she is a Brahmin. Look, she's coming here again."

"Come with me, you are going to see the doctor now," the girl said with a smile and holding out her hand.

Sheti was ushered into a bare-looking room where a white-haired, elderly man was sitting. He smiled at Sheti and she liked him at once. She looked with envy at the Nepali nurse in her smart blue sari and white cap.

The doctor now examined her and wrote various things down on a chart. When he had finished, he asked her if she had anyone with her so Sheti explained about Aunt Maya. When he heard that the aunt lived next door to Sheti he asked to see her too.

Maya felt very shy coming into the doctor's room and wondered what she should say. The doctor asked her about her family and she found herself telling him about her husband's recent death. He then asked Maya if he might examine her too.

As Sheti waited outside, her new Brahmin friend, whose name was Jyote, came over to her and said that the doctor wanted to have a blood test and a small section taken from her face. Sheti was very frightened and asked if she might wait until Maya joined her. So Jyote showed her where to go when their names were called and then left her.

Sheti sat in the Out-patients Department and watched the patients coming and going. Here was a man being carried in on a stretcher slung on a long pole. She heard them say he had fallen out of a tree some days ago. He certainly looked ill and battered. Over to her left an anxious looking mother sat with a very sick baby boy in her arms. Seeing Sheti's sympathetic glance she began to tell what had happened. He had high fever and the mother, desperate, had given him a dose of the local herbal medicine. "That was last night," she said, pulling her shawl more closely around the fretful child. "But this morning he was no better. Then I remembered that a neighbour of ours had brought her little boy to this Hospital. People had said there was no hope for him, but he got better here. So I've brought my baby."

The baby looked completely dehydrated but Sheti was neither surprised nor shocked to see the mother refuse to give him the water Jyote was offering her. It was not the custom to give water to a baby when he had a fever. But Sheti was glad to see that Jyote was doing all she could to get them in to the doctor as soon as possible.

Many people had, like Sheti and Maya, walked for days to get to the Hospital and Sheti heard many tales of happenings in the Hospital as she sat there awaiting her turn. An old lady came and sat beside her and cried as she told how her daughter's life had been saved. She had been in labour for four days and the Brahmin priest had said she would die, but a young man who had been in Baltichaur training as a teacher had urged them to bring her to the Hospital. The Brahmin had insisted that it was useless but, fearing more the disgrace and expense of having her die with a dead baby inside her, the husband had been persuaded to bring her in. The baby had been dead, but her daughter was all right and they had been told that she could have further children. The old lady kept wringing her hands and saying, "They are like gods here!"

Maya came out of Dr. Finley's room with a paper in her hand and said that she too had to have some tests done. Jyote came over and took the paper from Maya, and told her to wait until her name was called. Sheti was eager to know what Dr. Finley had said to Maya. Maya told how he had examined her and been particularly anxious about some patches she had on her back. "He asked me if I could feel anything when he stuck a pin into them, and, you know, I couldn't feel anything. I had wondered what those patches were, but they didn't hurt so I hadn't worried."

Sheti's name was called then and she went to the laboratory where they took a small section of skin from her face, and some blood. A little later Maya too went for tests.

While they waited to be called again to the doctor, they sat and talked, and some of the other patients talked too. To most of them everything was very strange as they had never been to a hospital before, but some people lived locally and said how now they never called the Brahmin, or the witch doctor, or used any of the old cures, but always came straight to hospital when they or any of their family were ill.

Sheti and Maya felt full of fear and apprehension as they sat there. What was to become of them? Would they be able to go home? Was there any cure for their disease? Would they die soon of it? These and other thoughts arose in their minds. It seemed a very long wait before Dr. Finley called them in to his consulting room. The nurse said that they might go in together.

Dr. Finley was very kind, and said that they had a disease that was curable, but that they would have to go on having treatment for a very long time. He would like, he said, if possible, for Sheti to stay in hospital so that he could keep

30

an eye on her, and get rid of the patches that were beginning to appear on her face. He would give Aunt Maya medicine, and she could go home and send Sheti's Mother in. Jyote would look after Sheti and see that she settled into the ward alright. He called Jyote and asked her to explain to Maya and Sheti what he wanted them to do.

Jyote took Sheti and Maya down to the ward, and showed them where Sheti would sleep if she stayed. Maya was in two minds about letting her stay, but as Jyote pointed out, if she went home they would have the continual anxiety of the village realising what was the matter with her—especially as the marks were on her face. Maya, if she kept up treatment, would have nothing to worry about, as her marks were only on her back. So after talking it over, Maya decided to leave Sheti, and take the news home, and get Santa Kumari to come in to see her.

Water supply with Fishtail Mountain in background

CHAPTER FIVE

IN Chisopani, Santa Kumari was talking to her daughter Chandri. "Oh, I wonder what has happened to Sheti, I do wish we could hear. So much has happened since she left; if only we could have news."

"Don't worry, Mother. Now Diwali is over, no doubt they will come in a day or two."

"Yes, Chandri, I know, and you have been very good staying on like this with me. You had better go home today. Man Bahadur is not strong and it is too much for him working the farm on his own."

"I don't like to leave you, but I think I had better get back. Man Bahadur has had a very bad cough recently." Santa Kumari sighed, then she said: "You'd better have your rice and curry, and then go."

"Yes, I think so, Mother."

Santa Kumari prepared the rice and curry for herself and Chandri on the open wood fire. After they had eaten, Chandri started off down the trail home, and Santa Kumari took up her water pot to fetch the daily supply from the well. The path led down through the village. As she came near to the school, she looked up and who should she see coming towards her but Maya.

"Maya, welcome home! What's happened? Where's Sheti?"

"She has stayed. She is all right. You go and get the water

and I'll go on up to the house. I hear Saraswati has died. You must have had an awful time."

"Yes, it has been terrible. You go on up. I'll come as quickly as I can."

It was not long before Santa Kumari was telling Maya of all that had happened to Saraswati; her death and cremation. Then Maya told of their visit to Baltichaur, of seeing the doctor and how he had told them that Sheti definitely had got leprosy. He wanted her to stay in hospital for a few months for treatment and then she could come home.

"Can she be cured?" Santa Kumari asked eagerly.

"Yes, the doctor said she could, but she would have to take tablets regularly. I didn't want to leave her but there was such a nice Brahmin girl, Jyote, about Sheti's own age, who said she would look after her until you could go in. She said, too, that you could stay with her for a few days there."

"A Brahmin to invite me! that's most unusual, isn't it?"

"Yes, but so many things were strange in that hospital, Santa Kumari. I must tell you something. The doctor examined me too and told me I have leprosy, but it is not the spreading type. I couldn't believe it when I heard. I thought maybe I couldn't understand properly what the white doctor was saying, but Jyote and another white lady explained to me afterwards that there are two types of leprosy; one spreads and the other doesn't. They explained that if I take medicine I won't get disfigured and there is no danger of anyone catching it from me. They told me leprosy is a disease and not as we have been taught, a curse from the gods. I can live in my own home. The doctor says if anyone makes any trouble he will give me a certificate with the Government stamp on it to show the headman. I heard from one of the other patients that Jyote and the white lady had actually gone out to her village to explain to the headman about her. I've been given these little white pills to take each day, and I can go again in six months".

"Where is Sheti?"

"She is in the hospital in a room with six beds in it. Jyote made arrangements with the hospital 'hotel' for her to have food until you arrive."

"What about money?"

"Well, I did leave some money for her food, and gave 10 rupees deposit for her treatment. I was able to collect what was left of Jarhu's pension, too, and they have promised to see if they can let me have some more. The white lady was very helpful over that too. She gave me a letter to take to the pensions office. By the way, I've got a book for Bhimsen."

"He will be pleased with that, he is always wanting books to read these days."

"Do you know, when Jyote told me that leprosy is not a curse she also read to me about someone—Jesus, she called Him—who healed leprosy. She told me He loves us and cares about us, and not to forget His name—JESUS. It has kept coming back to me on the journey home. Certainly, that doctor was very kind to both of us. One patient told me he had come over ten days' walk because he had heard about the new God in Baltichaur. No one had spoken to him or touched him for years, and he had been stoned from place to place. He was afraid to come. I saw him come in and he looked like a kicked dog, but he said when he went in to see the doctor, and he touched him, it almost made him weep, as it was so long since anyone had done so. A nice boy named Lal Bahadur talked to him and gave him some books to read. Lal went with him to the Governor to stamp a certificate which the doctor had given him to say he was having treatment and that no one was to stone him. He was so happy and eager to read the books Lal had given him, and has now gone back to his village. It will take him about twelve days walk. It's up near Mukti-nath."

"Well, I had better get ready to go in to see Sheti, hadn't I?"

"Yes, I think you should go tomorrow."

Washing in the pond

CHAPTER SIX

ONE evening, Jyote had a little leisure so she took the tape recorder and some tapes into the ward where the patients and their relatives were sitting chatting. She asked permission to play some religious songs to them and got a hearty response. Most of the tape recordings were of Nepali hymns set to Nepali tunes. The villagers loved their own little catchy lilts and were quick to learn both words and tune. Jyote knew that this was a most effective way of spreading the gospel, for many illiterate folk went back to remote village homes singing Bible verses and Christian truths.

For nearly an hour she taught the group to sing Bible verses to music they could pick up and remember. Closing her tape-recorder she offered books to all who could read, books which contained the Bible songs they had been hearing and trying to sing. Some of the teenage schoolboys bought them. Very few of the women could read but a few bought literature for their sons or brothers who were readers. Next Jyote produced a little pamphlet and said cheerfully: "Here is something you can all read; it is called the wordless book. See, page one is green—green for freshness, new life, the colour of the buds that reveal that a tree or bush is alive. Page two is black, the colour of darkness, of ignorance, of sin, of blindness. It is the colour of our hearts when we are far from God. Page three is red—it reminds us of the blood of the sacrifices we sometimes offer to the gods. Do you offer such sacrifices?"

There was a quick response from most of the little group. "We do! we do!" they said.

"When you offer a goat or a chicken to the gods, what does it do for you?" asked Jyote.

"It pleases the gods. They will know that we fear them and have not forgotten them. If they are in a good mood we may hope to get what we want and not be molested."

"Are the gods very powerful? Can they do everything? Do you love them?"

"Some are more powerful than others; some have power to destroy, some to give fertility, some to give prosperity and good luck."

"Which god do you love the most?"

Here there was a pause, then someone said: "It is difficult to say. We must try to keep them all happy."

"I am afraid of Kali," said another. "She visited my baby brother and he died of smallpox. The Brahmin priest said Kali was angry with the whole village and that she wanted a big sacrifice."

"What did the people do?" asked Jyote.

"Kali wanted an elephant and we had no live elephant up here in the mountains so the potters made one of clay. We all marched to Kali's shrine, carrying it and chanting her praises. The smallpox stopped then, but a lot of people died. What god do you follow, Jyote?"

"Oh, I am a Christian. A follower of the Lord Jesus Christ. My parents were Hindus and used to take sacrifices to the gods as you do, but there were things that troubled them. For instance, they wondered why the cow should be considered holy. Why it was a sin to kill or injure it, and not such a sin to injure a woman; and many other things. Everyone around seemed to be so full of fear. We lived then in a town on the border of Nepal, and white people came to live there. They ran a dispensary among the Nepalis and my parents used to go to them for medicine. There they heard for the first time about God who loved them so much that He died for them. My parents believed, became Christians, and were baptised. I was brought up to know about Jesus from the time I was small, but now I have come to accept Him and believe for myself that Jesus is the only true Saviour of the world, and that He died for my sin, and for each one of you. And I want more than anything else for you to know how much Jesus loves you.

"Do you know that for many years my parents prayed for this land that God would prepare hearts to hear about Jesus Christ because until the revolution in 1951 no Christians could live and work in Nepal.

"I am sorry, I have to go now, but here comes Lal Bahadur. He will take over the tape-recorder and tell you more. He has recently become a Christian, an answer, maybe, to the prayers of those who prayed when Nepal was a closed land. Come, Lal, you tell them, I must be off now."

"Would you really like to hear," said Lal, "or would you rather I played the tape-recorder?"

"No, do tell us," said the patients.

"I used to think," said Lal, "that Christianity was for western people only, not for us, but I know now that God loves the whole wide world and will save all who come to Him through His Son, Jesus Christ."

"How did you come to believe on this new God and His Son?"

"Have you heard the song 'Jesus, Name high over all'? That song really started the change in my life. As you know, everyone in the villages is afraid of evil spirits and demons. I was very troubled by a demon that appeared to me, and one day when I was going down to the bazaar from the hospital, there it was on the path in front of me. I didn't know what to do. Suddenly I remembered that in the hospital they had spoken of the power of the name of Jesus, and the line from one of the Christian songs came to my mind—'Devils fear and fly'—so I said to the demon: 'In the name of Jesus, leave me! Go away!" All I can say is that it went. This, as you may imagine, started me thinking. I can read, so when I got back to the hospital the next day I got hold of some of the books here, and as I read I became convinced that what I read was true. I've faced up to what it will mean to lose caste and to become an outcast Christian, for those who have become Christians in Tamgas have had a lot of trouble from the local officials. But in spite of this I have become a Christian. Now I have a peace in my heart such as I have never known before."

He was interrupted at this point as someone called his name.

"Oh, there is the doctor calling, I'll have to take the tape-recorder away and go now. If you would like to start learning to read, I'll ask Jyote if she can help you."

CHAPTER SEVEN

SANTA Kumari trudged up the last hill into Baltichaur. She was feeling afraid. What would it be like at the hospital? She wished she hadn't had to come alone, but Bhimsen had the farm to think of and it was difficult for him to get away. Nor could she expect Maya to come in again. All the same, she did feel frightened. So that big building on the top of the hill must be the hospital and she would have to ask the way out there when she got to the bazaar.

It took much longer than she had expected; it was nearly dusk when she eventually reached the hospital. She asked for Sheti and was shown where she would find her. Santa Kumari could hardly believe her eyes when she saw inside the ward with its beds, complete with pillows and sheets, for the patients to sleep on. She teased Sheti about it when she eventually found her.

"Mother, you won't be able to stay here the night. I'll go and find Jyote and see if you can stay with her. She said you could if you came. I think she's in Out-patients."

Jyote was in the Out-patients department and when Sheti asked if her mother could stay with her she was quite willing to have her.

"She will have to wait until I have finished here and then we can go home together," Jyote said. "I will bring her back with me tomorrow to see you."

Santa Kumari arrived early the next morning and Sheti

41

came out and sat on the ward verandah with her. Santa Kumari told her what had been happening in the village, chiefly about the death of Saraswati. Sheti told her mother what the doctor had said and how she would probably have to be in hospital a few months and then she would be able to go home. If she kept up her treatment she would get quite well. She told her mother that the doctor wanted to see her also and that Jyote would arrange it for her.

"Isn't Jyote nice?" she said. "And you must meet Lal Bahadur. His grandfather lives in our village. You know him, Mother, don't you? Salik Ram, he lives near the Mukhia's house."

"Yes, I know him. *Namastai,* Lal Bahadur."

"Namastai, Mother. Did you have a good journey? Sheti has been worrying about you, so it is good that you have come. She will have to stay a few months more and then she will be able to go home. Well, it has been nice to meet you, but I must get on with my work." And with a cheerful smile Lal went on his way to the Out-patient Department

"Mother, did Jyote talk to you at all last night about her religious beliefs?" asked Sheti when they were alone.

"Yes, but I couldn't understand much, though I must say the events of these last months have made me think—whether there is a stronger spirit than the one we know, and what happened to Saraswati after she died, and things like that. Still, one mustn't query, we have always gone to the temple and made our *'pujas';* that is the way for us, not this new fangled western religion."

"Do you know, Mother, Lal says it isn't the white man's religion, and that Jesus, about whom they speak, probably was not even white. Lal says that Jesus is God's way of salvation for us all, and we no longer have to worship idols and go on long pilgrimages. In fact, their holy book, the Bible, says it's wrong to worship idols."

"Well, it's all I have ever known, and I've always gone to the temple every festival, and certainly your father always did."

"Here comes Jyote, she has come to take you to see the doctor. Do not be afraid, Mother, he is very nice."

Dr. Finley examined Santa Kumari but found her to be free of any leprosy. He explained to her about Sheti, and how she would have to come in to the hospital from time to time for a check-up. Santa Kumari found herself telling the doctor all about the trouble they had in the village over Saraswati, and how they had hidden her husband Jarhu.

Dr. Finley listened sympathetically and said that Santa Kumari was to let him know if there was any trouble when Sheti went home. There was no need, he said, for them to tell the village that she had leprosy. If Sheti kept up treatment, the disease would not spread and no one in the village would be in danger of infection. If, however, she stopped treatment, it would be another story and it might even be necessary for him to tell the village elders.

Santa Kumari was rather overwhelmed by all the doctor told her, but Jyote and Sheti helped her afterwards to understand. After discussion it was decided that Santa Kumari should go home, and that Man Bahadur, her son-in-law should come in and collect Sheti in three months' time.

"I think Man Bahadur should see the doctor here, too, Mother, about his bad chest," Sheti said.

The day by day routine of the ward went on, the daily dressings, medicine giving, injections and doctor's rounds. Jyote or one of the sisters often brought the tape-recorder to the ward. Sheti enjoyed hearing the tapes. On Sundays and at other times she occasionally went with Jyote to services in the hospital chapel or in the home of one of the sisters or doctors. She was interested in what she heard, but certainly not convinced that it was the truth, though she had not much faith in Hinduism and did not know what she really believed, if anything.

One morning about three months later, Jyote heard Sheti calling her, "Jyote! Jyote! do come here, I want to tell you something."

"What is it, younger sister?"

"It is about the dream I had last night. I was in a crowd, like the meetings here. Someone was talking, and I did my best to get out. Then suddenly I was alone, and a figure stood in front of me and said my name—"Sheti". As I stood there, He lifted His hands, and turned them over to show me the palms, and He said: 'Sheti, I died for you, I am your Saviour!' and Jyote, do you know, as I looked I saw there were nail prints in His hands. I fell down before Him and said 'My Lord and my God'. Oh, Jyote, I've heard you singing here so often about Jesus calling and I know He called me last night in that dream. I now believe in Him."

"Oh, dear sister, isn't that wonderful! Praise God. Let us get the Bible and see what God says, because you know when you become a follower of the Lord Jesus you have to face persecution and difficulties. You must know how to be prepared for them."

"Jyote, I have got such a peace in my heart. I feel at the moment I could face anything. I feel even happy that I have leprosy as it has meant that I have met with Jesus."

"Look, Sheti, you have committed yourself to the Lord Jesus and He has, as He promised, accepted you. Jesus said 'Him that cometh to Me I will in no wise cast out' (John 6.37) 'Behold I stand at the door and knock; if any man opens the door I will come in' (Rev. 3.20). God says that the moment we take the Lord Jesus to be our Saviour we become His children. See, here in St. John 1.12, 'As many as received Him to them gave He power to become the sons or daughters of God.' If you ask Him, He will forgive your sins and give you that power. He will send His Holy Spirit to dwell in your heart, and His Spirit is greater than any of the spirits you will meet in the village when you go home.

"Remember, Sheti, He is able to keep you from falling. Let us have a time of prayer together and you tell Him in your own words how you have come to Him."

There, in the corner of the ward, the two girls prayed quietly together, Sheti haltingly speaking to her newly found Saviour and Friend.

44

"Here is Lal Bahadur, Sheti, tell him what has happened. The Bible says if you tell others with your own mouth that Jesus Christ is your Lord, and believe in your own heart that God has raised Him from the dead, you will be saved."

"Oh, Jyote, you are hard on me," Sheti said, laughing.

"But isn't that true, Sheti? Isn't that what you do believe?"

"Yes", said Sheti, looking shyly up at the boy she told him of her dream of the previous night and the change it had made in her life.

"Well you must really get on with your reading now, so you can read the Bible for yourself. We will let you have some books when you go home, and you can get people in the village to read them."

"I want to go and tell Mother, Aunt Maya, and the others too. You must teach me. I have so much to learn," said Sheti humbly.

Down to the valley and up to the Himalaya

CHAPTER EIGHT

SHETI'S time for leaving the hospital had come but Dr. Finley was not satisfied. Although she had responded to treatment, the patches on her face were still visible so it was decided she had better stay on for a further three months. She was able to get a message back to the village as Lal decided to go out to see his grandfather.

Sheti enjoyed being in hospital and was soon able to do jobs to help the nurses, such as making cotton wool balls for swabs. She also went on learning to read with Jyote and she was soon able to read for herself.

The six months were nearly up when one morning she heard Jyote calling her. "Sheti, here is your brother-in-law, Man Bahadur, come for you."

"Has he come for me? I thought Aunt Maya would have come as it is her time to see Dr. Finley again."

"No, it is your brother-in-law. He doesn't look at all well."

"He isn't strong and I know Mother is worried about him. Do you think the doctor would see him?"

"Well, I expect Dr. Finley will like to see him, if only to check up that he has not got leprosy. If he finds anything wrong with his chest he can refer him for X-ray."

"*Namastai*, brother-in-law, how are you? How are Chandri and the children, and Mother?" said Sheti as Man Bahadur came forward.

47

"Namastai! They are all well," he replied, smiling at her. "When can you come home?"

"I don't know, we will have to see Dr. Finley and find out. Jyote is making an appointment for you to see him."

"What a big hospital this is. I never knew anything like this existed in our country."

"Yes, it is amazing. Even so, I am happy that I can go home."

Sheti enquired why Aunt Maya had not come and Man Bahadur told her that she did not feel it was necessary for her to fetch medicine as she still had a few tablets left, and she was busy. Sheti was worried, for she realised that if this was so it meant that her aunt had not been taking the tablets regularly. She did not, however, tell Man Bahadur this, and was glad when she could say to him: "Here is Jyote, you can go and see Dr. Finley now."

Man Bahadur went to the out-patients department where Dr. Finley examined him. The doctor found he had no leprosy but he was concerned about his chest and, therefore, sent him for an X-ray and blood tests.

Later, Dr. Finley said, "Man Bahadur, I am very concerned about the condition of your chest. Have you heard of tuberculosis? You have that disease. See here on this X-ray, it shows that you have it badly in one lung and a patch on the other."

"Doctor, what does this mean?"

"It means that you must go very carefully. You must not do heavy work, and you must take medicine for a very long time."

"But doctor, how can I manage? I have to work my farm."

"Yes, I realise that, but really I should admit you to hospital, and that would be even more diffcult for you. I would like you to go and talk it over in our social work department with Sister Molly and Jyote, whom I think you have already met. They will discuss things with you, as to how best you can meet some of your problems. I have dis-

Bridge over Mardi River and Machhapuchare (23,000ft.)

Marsyangdi River west of Mugling on Kathmandu to Pokhara road

*Annapurna II (26,041ft.) and Lamjung Himal (22,900ft.)
from Kalikathan ridge, east of Pokhara*

Begnas lake and Himalchuli (25,890ft.)

Begnas Lake and Annapurna Range, east of Pokhara.
Annapurna I (left) (26,500ft.) Machhapuchare (right) (23,000ft.)

Children near Pachabaiya School

Annapurna II (26,041ft.)

Bearers south of Pokhara

charged Sheti. You can take her home. She will have to come back to see me in six months' time but I would like you to come again in two months. Now nurse will show you where to go."

Man Bahadur was shown out of the doctor's room and into the medical social worker's office.

Sister Molly greeted him. *"Namastai,* Man Bahadur. It is good to meet you. We heard about you and your family from Sheti and we are pleased that you have come to take her home. She told us you had not been well and had this troublesome cough."

"Yes, I have a cough, but I did not think it was very serious."

"Well, I am afraid it is, Man Bahadur. I expect Dr. Finley told you that you will have to take medicines for several years, and come in here periodically for check-ups."

"Yes, he did."

"Who is at home? You have a wife and children?"

"Yes, a wife and two boys—Daman is thirteen and Jit eleven—And I have a daughter aged nine. They all go to school."

"You have a small farm?"

"We have our own farm, and also help my sister-in-law who lives next door. My brother works down in India. They have only one son, Paul Singh, aged fourteen and a married daughter."

"Your wife helps you with the farm, does she? You understand do you, Man Bahadur, that doctor does not want you to do any of the heavy work on the farm? I realise that this is difficult for you, but maybe your elder son and Paul Singh can help you. What is your brother doing in India? Is there any possibility of his coming home to work?"

"My brother is in the railway in India and he may be on leave in a few months time. He helps when he is home."

"At present you are spreading germs in your sputum. As there is a danger for your family you should try to have a separate plate and drinking vessel, and do not let your family

49

eat food off your plate. Don't spit around; make a leaf plate and learn to spit into that, and then burn it. You have a buffalo, haven't you? Try and drink as much milk as you can. Boil it before you drink it, and don't drink cow's milk."

Sister Molly and Jyote talked on with Man Bahadur, making sure he understood how to take his medicine and the importance of keeping up the treatment when, in all probability, in a few months he would begin to feel a little better. His diet and the running of his farm was also discussed. Jyote then arranged for Sheti's discharge and at last the moment for their departure came.

"Well, goodbye, Sheti, don't forget to take your tablets and remember what you have learnt here. You don't go alone; Jesus will never leave you or forsake you, and we will be praying for you. Don't be surprised if one day Sister Molly and I turn up on your doorstep."

"Namastai, older sister. Pray for me and I'll pray you will be able to visit us in our homes."

On the trail trekking home together Sheti told Man Bahadur about the teaching concerning the Christian religion and the Lord Jesus Christ she had heard while she was in hospital.

Man Bahadur listened patiently and said he had heard about Christ when he had served in a Gurkha regiment.

"You know, Sheti, I believe that there are many roads to God, and Jesus Christ is just one of them. We have Lord Shiva, Vishnu, Kali and the others; the Christians have Christ, the Buddhists, Buddha, and the Muslims their prophet Mohammad. All think theirs is the right way to bring men to God. In each philosophy there is good teaching and we can learn a lot from the Buddhists and Muslims. I once read some of the teaching of Christ—Ratna in our village had it in his college course—a sermon on a hill or something it was called, and I thought at the time if men really lived like that it would make a lot of difference, even in our village. But you know that it is against the law of this land for anyone to change their religion. We all have to continue in the traditions of our forefathers."

"But don't you think, brother-in-law, that changes are coming? A lot of young fellows do not really believe in the old gods, do they?"

"No, they may say that when they are together, but not many will go against the witch doctor and the priests. And don't they all take part in the festivals, even if it is mostly the drinking and gambling? Our country is based on the keeping of Hindu laws; the King retains his power because he is said to be an incarnation of Vishnu."

It was very hot and it took them over a day and a half to get back to the village, and so they had plenty of time to talk. Sheti discovered that her brother-in-law knew quite a lot about Christianity, though he had never spoken of it at home. He had not thought of the possibility of becoming a Christian himself. He had always felt that Hinduism was his and his country's religion and that it was right for him. He knew that some had become very interested when they were in the army and had even become Christians. He told Sheti how one of his friends had actually been baptised and so made a complete break with Hinduism. He had gone home so full of desire to tell his family, hoping to persuade them to accept Christianity. He had, however, hardly reached his village when his father, who had been ill, died. He was the eldest son, and therefore, by Hindu custom, obliged to shave his head and perform ceremonies which would assure his father a good place in the next life. This friend, Man Bahadur explained to Sheti, had only just come home, and not liking to upset his mother further by telling her immediately of his new found faith, had gone through the ceremonies, and afterwards he said he had a tremendous sense of guilt that he had gone back on his Christianity. He had not been able then to confess his new-found faith and gradually the months and years had gone by and he never told the village at all. Man Bahadur said he knew all this because he had asked his friend about it when he himself came out of the army and had found him back in Hinduism, much to his surprise.

Sheti was amazed that her brother-in-law knew so much, for he had never spoken of it. She asked him why he had not mentioned hearing about Christianity and he said that he had not thought it important. And he had not been very impressed with the lives of the Christians he had met.

Sheti wondered how her mother and her other relatives would react when she told them of her dream, and how she was now a Christian.

Man Bahadur's advice to her was not to say too much. There was no reason, he argued, why she shouldn't believe in Christ in her heart and follow Christian precepts if she wanted to. It would be wisest not to break with the old traditions. She could still go to the temple and worship in the name of Christ. It would be better not to tell anyone. "One day," Man Bahadur said, "we might have freedom of religion in our country, but until then it would be better to remain quiet."

CHAPTER NINE

IT was a hot journey back to Chisopani for Man Bahadur and Sheti and they felt very weary as they trudged up the last three miles of the trail to Sheti's home.

Maya was cleaning her cooking pots as they arrived. They greeted her and sat down on the verandah. "Where is Mother?" Sheti asked.

"She's still out with the goats but she won't be long now as she is expecting you."

"I'll go and meet her and perhaps I can help her bring in some grass for them."

Sheti went out to meet her mother and found her with the goats down in the jungle near their water spring. Santa Kumari was, of course, delighted to see her daughter again and Sheti told her the news from the hospital, that Dr. Finley did not want her to go in to see him for another six months. When they got back to the house, and after they had had a meal, Man Bahadur went home. Sheti gave her mother a new sari she had bought in Baltichaur.

Sheti knew that her mother was very pleased to see her and to get the news from the hospital but she also knew there was something worrying her. "Is something the matter, Mother?" she asked.

"There has been some trouble here since you went, Sheti,"

her mother replied. "Everyone is very worried about the drought, about the cause of it. They are arranging a special ceremony to pray for rain. Bhimsen and Juthe are going. Certainly the gods must be angry. If not why is there such a shortage of water? The crops are just withering up; if we don't get rain soon I don't know what we will do. It will be very hard on everyone and there will be famine."

The next day Sheti, Santa Kumari and Maya watched Bhimsen and Juthe set out with drums and a trumpet, prepared to join the procession round the village to call on the gods for rain. The villagers shouted again and again as they marched—"Oh, Great God send rain! Great God, send rain!" They went to the temple on the hill where the priests performed ceremonies to placate the gods and to find out who might be responsible for the drought.

Early next morning Bhimsen and Juthe returned home, and waking Santa Kumari told her that the priests were saying that old Lillawatti was a witch.

"What's that? what's that?" said Santa Kumari, "Lillawatti a witch? That is ridiculous, she can't be. We have known her all our lives. She has always lived peaceably and quietly in the village. There is no harm in the old soul. What are they going to do to her?"

"They are today going to tell her that she can't go to the well for her water, and no one is to associate with her. Then they are going to have a village council meeting to decide what to do next."

"Oh, it's a shame, that old lady would not hurt a fly. I cannot believe that she is in any way responsible for the drought. It's a ruse to get her land."

"You be careful what you say, Mother, we don't want them picking on you."

"Well, her land goes to old Ram Bhakta. I wonder what he will do when he hears this news. Poor old lady, to have this happen at her time of life. She must be four twenties and six years at least. I must go over and see her."

"Mother, you must not go near her."

"Oh, I know the time to go when there is no one about. I must see her, she is no more a witch than I am, I'm sure."

*   *   *

Some time later Man Bahadur came to Santa Kumari. *"Namastai,* Mother."

"Namastai, son-in-law."

"What is the latest news about Lillawatti? Bhimsen told me what happened last week. Just now she greeted me; she is still in her home, I see."

"Yes, as you know, the rain came. The priests went to her house and had a ceremony to cast out the evil spirits and to warn Lillawatti to keep free from witchcraft. Poor old soul, I heard she had to pay them over a hundred rupees for that and I also heard that Ram Bhakta gave the village council several hundred rupees. No one quite knows how much. This has all very much shaken old Lillawatti. I saw her today and she was pleased to hear Sheti has come back home. The whole village is in bondage because of the fear of witchcraft and this drives them to be cruel to old people like Lillawatti."

A Hindu temple

CHAPTER TEN

SHETI found it difficult to settle back into the life of the village after being away for so long. There was not too much comment as to why she had been at Baltichaur. The hospital there was a general one and not for leprosy cases only. The villagers knew that people went there for all types of disease and stayed for varying lengths of time. Sheti was, however, very worried about Aunt Maya. She had finished her tablets but because she showed, to her way of thinking, no worrying symptoms of leprosy she just did not see the necessity of taking the long trek into Baltichaur for a check-up. Sheti tried to persuade her, but it was no use.

Both Santa Kumari and Maya were thrilled to hear Sheti read and so each day she read to them from simplified copies of the Gospels she had brought with her from the hospital. Bhimsen took some of them too, to read for himself. So the weeks passed quickly for Sheti. She was working in the fields with the maize crop and fetching the water from the spring each day; cutting fodder for the buffalo and taking the goats out to find pasture. People were naturally interested to hear about the hospital and so Sheti was able to talk about the life there and tell about the meetings and hymn singing. She had brought back with her a hymn book, so she sat and sang these songs for the villagers. She had a pleasant voice and as the tunes were easily picked up the people enjoyed sitting and singing with her. This led on to

57

people asking about the words of the hymns so Sheti found she had opportunity to talk of her newly found faith.

One evening Sheti was sitting singing on the verandah when she heard a call. Looking up, who should she see coming up the path but Jyote and Sister Molly, and a little way behind them Lal Bahadur carrying a basket on his back. *"Namastai,* Sheti! Is there a sleeping place to be found here or not?"

Sheti laughed. *"Namastai!* Of course, come and sit down. How are you? How is everyone at the hospital?"

Soon they were exchanging news and Santa Kumari was bustling around getting a meal from rice out of Lal Bahadur's basket.

During the meal, villagers came up to enquire who the visitors were. They stayed to stare at Sister Molly who seemed strange to them with her fair hair and blue eyes. Jyote, too, amazed them. Obviously a Brahmin, what was she doing travelling the hills with a white woman and sitting to eat with such as Santa Kumari? After supper Jyote suggested that they should sing hymns. "We have a portable tape-recorder with us and we could play that and perhaps some of the folk here would like to listen."

"Yes, I am sure they would" Sheti said as she got out her hymn book. Soon they were sitting on the verandah singing the hymns that she had learnt while in hospital, and in the dusk more and more people gathered to listen. At the end Lal Bahadur took the opportunity to tell them of his new found faith in Christ. The villagers listened well and asked questions afterwards. There was bright moonlight so people didn't mind staying on, and it was late when at last they were all able to settle down for the night.

Next morning Sister Molly and Jyote asked after Maya and enquired why she had not been back to hospital. Maya said how busy she had been and how she did not see the need for going on with the treatment.

Sister Molly and Jyote explained to her the danger of the disease spreading in her body and how she would need to

58

take tablets for many years to make certain that the disease was no longer active. Maya at last agreed that she would go back with them to see Dr. Finley.

Lal Bahadur talked to Sheti about her faith, asking how she had got on since she came home. Sheti told him about Man Bahadur's knowledge of Christianity which he had hidden for so long, so Lal decided to go down and visit Man Bahadur and Chandri in their own home.

It was getting dusk when Lal arrived at Man Bahadur's house after his three hour trek down the hillside.

"Namastai!" he called, as Man Bahadur appeared.

The older man's face lit up as he saw him. *"Namastai,* Lal Bahadur! Where have you come from? Have you seen Sheti and Santa Kumari?"

"Yes, I have come from their home today. How are you, brother? You look much better."

"I am feeling better. Do come in and sit down."

Soon they were chatting round the open wood fire. Lal telling about the hospital and Man Bahadur about life in the village. He mentioned that there was a scare of smallpox in the area and that the priest had put a shrine at the entrance of the village to protect them. "Having been to hospital and been abroad, I personally haven't any faith in these things now," said he. Lal Bahadur was soon telling him of his own faith and they listened to the recorded Gospel messages and hymns on the tape that Lal had with him. Man Bahadur was very interested to see the tape-recorder and listened to the message. Chandri and the boys, and Paul Singh and his mother, and two neighbours, also came to listen.

"It's strange that whenever I hear anything Christian it seems to bring a peace in my heart," Man Bahadur said.

"Yes," agreed Chandri. "It seems to speak right inside you, does it not?"

"That is because they are the words of the true and living God," Lal Bahadur said. "He went to speak His words to all of us. We have to open our hearts to listen to Him."

59

"Please play more for us, and sing too," the others said.

As he played Lal noticed a man slip on to the end of the verandah and sit listening. Man Bahadur did not appear to notice him and so Lal went on playing and singing, and after a time the man went away.

It was dark when the neighbours went home and Man Bahadur and Lal got out the rice straw mats on which to sleep for the night.

"Who was the visitor on the verandah?" Lal asked. "That was Bishnu Ratna. He lives in the big house just above us. He's been in India for a number of years and has only recently come home. He's not, I am afraid, very friendly disposed towards us. He tried to trick me out of some land a little while ago but I went to the district office in Malpur and was able to prove it was mine. I've got the deeds here, but Bishnu Ratna was not pleased. By the way, Lal, I heard that when you become a Christian your right to hold land is taken from you. Is that so?"

"Yes, in some cases this has happened. I know a widow who has become a Christian and the local panchyat have ruled that she cannot continue to hold her husband's land."

"You know, Lal, I have thought that I would like to become a Christian, but if I did I fear they would take away my land and then what would my son, Daman, do if I had no land to leave him? We have no money or livelihood apart from our land. Also my father is still alive and he will expect me, as the oldest son, to do the last Hindu rites for him at his death. He puts complete faith in these for his position in the next life, and I know if I became a Christian I could not do them for him. If I was on my own as you are I think I might become a Christian; the more I hear of Christianity the more it seems to me to be the truth."

"Yes, it certainly is very hard for anyone of us in this land to become a Christian. Also if anyone likes to report us we could be put in jail. But Jesus Christ said that we should suffer for the sake of the Gospel, and that we are blessed if we do so. I know that I have been much jeered at, and called false to my country and people since I became a Christian, but I know also that I have never had such peace and purpose in my life. You know, brother, if you hear the voice of Jesus calling you, you must obey and follow Him." Man Bahadur looked troubled. "I feel there is so much yet that I need to know and understand before I could take such a step," he said.

"Yes, I realise that, but from being at Sheti's, I understand there are quite a few of you in whose lives the Spirit of God is working. I wonder if Pastor Dhanraj from Baltichaur could come and stay for a week, then you could hear more and ask him questions?"

"I would like that. I was very impressed with the old man when I saw him at the hospital, and I would like an opportunity to talk more with him—I think others would too. He could stay up at Santa Kumari's."

"Well, I think Maya is coming back with us to hospital so we can discuss it with the Pastor and then send a message back with her if and when he could come."

"Yes, that's a good idea. I could perhaps bring him back when I go in for my next check-up with Dr. Finley."

A hill town scene

CHAPTER ELEVEN

ONE evening some months later, the hymn singing in the village was over and Pastor Dhanraj was speaking to the group sitting on the floor in Santa Kumari's house. He was a tall, impressive looking man, taller than average for a Nepali, and one who had known in his own life the cost of following Christ. Brought up in a high caste Hindu home, he had been set for a successful business life in a city in India, until one day in the bazaar he had paused to listen to an open air preacher. The words of the man had so gripped him that he had gone back night after night to hear him, gradually realising the claims of Christ on his life. He had been baptised and consequently turned out by his wealthy family. He became an itinerant preacher and later pastor of a Nepali Church in the Assam hills. In 1952 when, as the result of a revolution in Nepal, the King took over power from the ruling Ranas, and Nepal was opened to foreigners, he had gone into Baltichaur with a party of missionaries and Nepali Christians.

His heart burned with love for his Saviour, and as he looked now around the group he spoke with great love and fervour of the sacrifice of Christ on Calvary for each one of them, and of His risen life. He preached the Lordship of Christ and the need for a complete break with idols, and obedience to the Saviour in being baptised.

It was difficult to tell, by looking, what was going on in

the hearts of those listening. Some, like Bhimsen and Juthe, seemed to be paying hardly any attention; Santa Kumari appeared to be asleep. Sheti, however, had her eyes fixed all the time on his face and was drinking in every word. Chandri, Man Bahadur and Maya were obviously listening too and from time to time nodded their heads in agreement. Bhimsen's wife's main occupation appeared to be the feeding of her baby. Pastor Dhanraj was, however, experienced enough to wait his time and let the Holy Spirit do His work in hearts, so he closed the meeting with prayer. The neighbours then slipped quietly away home and the rest spread out the rice mats to sleep on the floor at Santa Kumari's.

Next day, as he sat praying and reading his Bible on the verandah the pastor was not surprised to have first Sheti, and then Bhimsen and his wife Putali, come to talk to him, all expressing their desire to follow Christ and asking for baptism. Dhanaraj spoke to them of the meaning of this step in their lives and the possibility of persecution and even imprisonment. Seeing, however, that they were determined to confess their new faith whatever the cost might be, he discussed with them where and when the baptismal service could take place. It was decided that it should be in a week's time at a quiet spot in a nearby stream.

The pastor continued to have meetings each evening that week, giving special teaching to Sheti, Bhimsen and Putali. After two days Maya joined them. Santa Kumari said little but did not come to the meetings, and Juthe stopped attending the evening meetings. Others who had been interested, dropped off, but it was obvious that a great battle was going on in the hearts of Man Bahadur and Chandri. On the night before the baptism, after Dhanraj spoke of the claims of Christ on their lives, and the folly of such excuses as 'suffer me first to go and bury my father', quietly they came to him and asked him to baptise them too on the morrow.

It was a very joyful little company that set out the next day for the river. Sheti's only sadness was that her mother was not one with them. Santa Kumari had absolutely refused, though she did not oppose Sheti. She watched them go, and went back to prepare a meal for them on their return from the river.

So Sheti, Man Bahadur, Chandri, Bhimsen, Putali and Maya went through the waters of baptism at Chisopani, the first to stand for Christ in their district of Nepal. Dhanraj spoke afterwards of the need for them to put on the whole armour of God and to have regular prayer and Bible study. They then went to Man Bahadur's and Chandri's for their first communion service before climbing back up to Santa Kumari's house for their rice meal.

The next day Pastor Dhanraj had to go back to Balti-chaur, and it was with some rather anxious feelings that the little group said goodbye to him. Dhanraj, as he set out, had a heart full of praise for these men and women who were facing possible persecution for their faith. "God keep me true to them in prayer," he murmured.

After their baptism the group met whenever possible for Bible study and prayer. As they took their goats out to graze or cleaned their pots and pans, or worked in the fields, they thought and talked about the one true God and their new found faith. When they could, they spoke to their neighbours and friends also. The news that they had become Christians got about and they were subject for much discussion in the village.

Several of them were threatened by local officials that unless they returned to Hinduism they would be put in jail. They all knew that should an adverse report be sent into the district office about them, this could really happen.

Sheti found herself lying awake at night and pondering what it would be like. She sometimes felt very afraid and wondered if she would be able to stand firm for her faith in Christ if they were to take her. She thought of the stories she had heard of Daniel in the lions' den, and prayed that as the lion's mouth had been stopped so would the mouths of the officials be closed by God.

However, one Sunday when Bhimsen, Putali, Sheti and Maya were waiting for Man Bahadur and Chandri to come for prayer at the usual time, they did not arrive. They wondered what had happened and if some accident had befallen them, and as the hours slipped by and they still did not come, they became more and more anxious. Bhimsen was thinking of going to their home when Chandri arrived, carrying her water pot.

"*Namastai,* sister, whatever has happened?" they all asked as soon as Chandri had lowered her water pot and basket off her back at the edge of the verandah.

"Why didn't you come for service this morning? Where's Man Bahadur, is he all right?" were the questions they flung at her.

"Yes, he's all right," said Chandri. "We were on our way to the service when we met our local headman and others on the road, and they forbade us to come up to the service. They must have heard about it and watched us coming for several weeks, as they picketed the road on the route we came. They said if we persist in coming they will report us to the officials at Malpur. We didn't feel there was any point in antagonising them any further, so we went back home, but as soon as I could I went down for the water and slipped up here through the paths in the jungle. Man Bahadur wonders what we should do, as they obviously mean business and will watch the road for several weeks now."

"Well," said Bhimsen, "we will have a time of prayer now you have come, and ask God to guide us as to what we should do in the future. It would seem that we shouldn't give up meeting as we need the fellowship of each other and also the Bible says we are not to neglect the assembling of ourselves together!"

Maya chimed in, "I do not see how they can stop us meeting, as we are relatives and friends anyway, and there is no law against relatives meeting!"

"We will just have to be a bit more discreet for a week or two, that's all," rejoined Bhimsen, "and hope that it will blow over, but let's get out our New Testaments now and pray."

66

CHAPTER TWELVE

IT was some weeks later when Santa Kumari returned early one morning from collecting her water, to find Bhimsen letting out their goats. He was very distressed. "Mother" he said, "I don't know what is wrong with them but they all appear to be ill. Do you think is can be something they have eaten?"

"I wouldn't think so. But I didn't feed them last night; ask Sheti, she gave them their food and took them out to graze yesterday."

Sheti was called, but she could give them no explanation as to why the goats all seemed so ill. They decided, however, to give them a mixture of herbal medicine which had often helped in the past when they were not well. It did no good, and as the day passed they got worse. Sheti, Maya and Bhimsen had to take it in turns to be up with them all night, but try what they would, nothing they could do seemed to help the poor animals. Next day one by one they all died.

The little group was stunned and puzzled, and it was not until Santa Kumari came back from the village later on, that light began to dawn on them.

Santa Kumari reported that everyone in the village was discussing their loss and that the officials and others were losing no time to point out how the wrath of the gods had come upon them because they had become Christians. "You mark our words," they said to one another, "it doesn't do to meddle with these new fangled western religions. What was good enough for our ancestors is good enough for us."

As they were sitting there on the verandah, several of the village women came in to see and to commiserate with them on the death of the goats. They were all inclined to be a little superior and definitely blamed the loss of the animals on the fact that Maya, Bhimsen, Putali and Sheti had become Christians. None, however, had known goats die as these had done. It seemed strange that they were all so fit and well when Sheti had taken them out two days ago and now they were all dead!

It was Juthe, listening to the conversation of the women and others in the village, who eventually came out with the suggestion that they might have been poisoned.

Man Bahadur and Chandri continued in spite of the pickets to come up through the back ways of the jungle, to join with the others for worship, and it was with great joy that they were able to report that their next door neighbours were now coming to join them for prayer each day, and had expressed a desire to be Christians. Also another distant relative of Chandri had been to stay with them. She had heard about Christianity through another relative and had long been interested. She had been recently widowed, and she hoped to be able to come and join them at their service next Sunday. Her two sons were in the army.

This news heartened the little group. For they had had many pressures on them in recent weeks, and they were still feeling severely the loss of the goats.

They read together the verses in Matthew 5 and in 1 Peter 3 about being happy when, because of being followers of Jesus, they were reviled and persecuted and lied about. Sometimes they felt comforted, but often they felt scared too. They encouraged each other by telling how God was teaching them, and how the ways God had helped them in their individual problems. They found that the outside persecution drew them closer to each other, and they learned to look to the Lord for answers much more than they had ever done when things were easier.

Sheti was troubled about the future. She realised that by becoming a Christian she had broken the usual pattern for girls of her age whose parents would normally arrange a marriage for them. Though, as she had leprosy, it would have been difficult for her mother to find a husband for her anyway. Two of her friends had recently been married to men they had never met, who lived in villages about five hours' walk from Chisopani. They had not known anything about the arranged marriages until the relatives had arrived from their future husbands' villages to take them there. She had watched them go off crying, and had wondered if they were following the traditional pattern of weeping as they went, or if they really had been sad and afraid to go. One was now reported to be very happy, but the other had arrived home to her mother this very week saying the would not stay with her husband. She had been forcibly taken back to him.

Sheti thought of them both now, knowing that the greatest hope in their lives would be to have a son, and thereby have an heir, and also be more likely to keep their husbands from taking another wife. Sheti supposed that now she was a Christian she would have little chance of marrying, and wondered whether God really did give His highest blessing when He gave a son?

Sheti pondered these things in her mind, and also the fact that she might have to go to jail. She had learnt the Bible verse when she was in hospital—'All things work together for good to them that love God, and are called according to His purpose.' Could things really work together for good if she had to go to jail? How would she stand up to it if it did happen? She had heard that conditions in the jail were awful. No sanitation, and everyone on top of each other; frequent quarrels, complete lack of privacy. Since being at the hospital she had come to appreciate these amenities more. Would people find out she had leprosy and make things even more difficult for her? Certainly she had no signs now. She was not infectious, and no one in the village seemed to be suspicious, but one never knew, it might leak out. It was a good thing treatment was easy, just a white pill to take each day. She would be able to continue that wherever she was.

The group of believers all went on with their day-to-day work, but they were more and more troubled by the ominous rumours that were increasing.

Sheti and Maya were out looking after the goats one day, when who should they see but Man Bahadur coming up over the hillside. After they had greeted him, he told them that their local headman had come with a paper from Malpur asking for the names of all who had been baptised with him. "I didn't know what to do, but felt that as it was a government order I had to give your names," Man Bahadur said. "I wonder now if I should not have done so."

"Oh you had to do so, brother, and now what do you think will happen?"

"I don't know, but they were taking the papers back to Malpur so it depends on the officials there whether we hear anything further or not. I haven't told Bhimsen and Putali yet. We had better get together, have some prayer and decide what we are going to do if they come for us. We must not involve the Baltichaur folk if possible—I have already had to give Pastor Dhanraj's name, as they insisted on knowing who had baptised us. I would send him a message, only he's away now, and anyway it may all come to nothing."

Three days passed, and there was no news, but on the morning of the fourth day two policemen arrived in the village with warrants for the arrest of Maya, Bhimsen, Putali, Sheti, Man Bahadur and Chandri. They had hastily to pack their few belongings and go with them to Malpur, after asking Santa Kumari to send Juthe in to Baltichaur as soon as possible to give them the news.

CHAPTER THIRTEEN

NEXT morning Dhanraj heard his wife calling him. "Father, come here quickly! There is a lad, Maya's son from Chisopani, here."

"*Namastai*, son. How are they in Chisopani?"

"*Namastai*, father, they are all well. The police, however, have come with warrants and have taken my mother, Bhimsen, Putali, Sheti, Man Bahadur and Chandri to the district office for questioning. Santa Kumari is beside herself and sent me in immediately to give you news, as they apparently have a warrant out for your arrest too."

"What is the charge against them?"

"That they have changed their religion from the Hindu faith and have been baptised. Against you it is said you have baptised them and forced them to become Christians."

"Where are they now—in Malpur? I must go to them at once."

"You had better not do that, they are sure to put you in prison. Maya said to tell you quickly so that you can go away now over the border to India."

Pastor Dhanraj's wife, hearing the conversation, said, "Oh, do let's go. It will mean six years in prison if you go to Malpur. That's the penalty, you know, for anyone found guilty of baptising people in Nepal."

"I know," Dhanraj said tenderly, "but these are my children in the Lord and I must go to them. Will you come with me, Juthe?"

"No, I must get back to Santa Kumari. Won't Lal go with you?"

"Yes, I expect he will. I must give news to them up at the hospital and get them praying. I will leave first thing tomorrow morning for Malpur."

So early next day saw Lal and Dhanraj setting off for Malpur. It was noon when they got there and Dhanraj went straight to the district office to ask about the Christians. He found them in the police station awaiting the arrival of the magistrate. When the police official heard the pastor's name he told him that there was a warrant out for his arrest. He drew aside and advised him not to stay and try to help the six but to get out of the country to India as soon as he could. Dhanraj discovered that the officer himself came from Darjeeling and, therefore, knew about Christianity and was not unsympathetic.

Dhanraj, however, was quite adamant in his decision. He must stay. Then he requested to see the prisoners. Seeing it was useless to refuse him he was allowed to join them.

He found them in good heart and encouraging one another in the Lord. They told him of the coming of the policeman and their arrest.

Man Bahadur had his Bible open at Matthew 10:19 and was reading to them: "When you are arrested, don't worry about what to say at your trial for you will be given the right words at the right time. For it won't be you doing the talking, it will be the Spirit of your Heavenly Father speaking through you." Dhanraj felt proud, as he heard them. They greeted him with obvious delight, only the two younger women, Chandri and Putali, were a little down. Putali had her baby in her arms and Chandri was obviously worrying about the two boys that she had had to leave with her sister-in-law.

As they were sitting talking, a police officer came in with cups of tea for them all. Before they drank the tea they all bowed their heads and Pastor Dhanraj gave thanks and prayed for them all. The police officer stood watching them all the time and when they took the tea to drink he said: "I can see you are all real Christians; that cup of tea was given you to test you to see if you would give thanks for it."

Shortly after this Man Bahadur, Chandri, Sheti, Maya, Bhimsen and Putali were called one by one before the magistrate. He cross-questioned them in turn about becoming Christians. When Sheti mentioned being in hospital in Baltichaur, the magistrate said he supposed the white people there had given her money to become a Christian. She denied this.

The magistrate told them all that if they insisted on saying that they were Christians he could have no alternative but to sentence them, according to the law of Nepal, to one year's imprisonment for changing their religion. He called them all together and spoke to them, saying he understood they wanted to be Christians, but he advised them to say in the court that they were Hindus; they could continue to believe in Christ in their hearts and just carry on outwardly the Hindu ceremonies. This would be denying Christ with their mouths but could they not still go on believing Him in their hearts? He then sent them away to consider their decision and told them to report at the court at 10 a.m. the next day.

That evening they all went back to Baltichaur with the pastor and gathered there for prayer. Pastor Dhanraj sought to strengthen their hearts. He reminded them of Christ's own words: "Whosoever will deny Me before men, him will I deny before My Father in heaven, and whosoever shall confess Me before men, him will I confess before My Father in heaven."

The group was very quiet when they set out for the court next day; many were the words of comfort and blessing given them by the believers in Baltichaur as they set out. When they arrived at the court who should they see but Ratna, Man Bahadur's enemy. Lal, who had gone with them, caught sight of him and said to Man Bahadur: "Isn't that Ratna, your next door neighbour?"

"Yes, it's him all right, and I believe it's because of him we are here. He reported me to the police. He found out I had become a Christian and thought it was a good way to get even with me over the land."

"Oh he did, did he? I wondered who had reported on you."

"He is looking our way; won't he gloat when you go to jail?"

"Yes, when I look at him I find it very difficult to obey Christ's words to love my enemies!"

It was getting on for 12 noon when they were called one by one to the magistrate. He asked them each by turn if they were Christian or Hindu, and if they intended to remain as baptised Christians or return to the traditions of their forefathers.

One by one they stood before the magistrate and declared their faith in Christ, but when it came to Maya's turn she faltered, burst into tears and said, "I am a Hindu." The magistrate passed sentence of one year's imprisonment on Sheti, Bhimsen, Chandri, Man Bahadur and Putali, and told Maya to report again in one month's time.

Pastor Dhanraj and Lal were waiting outside the court as the five came out in the custody of the police. Dhanraj's eyes filled with tears as they, with heads held high, walked past him on their way to jail, Putali carrying her young baby in her arms. As Chandri passed, one of the women in the crowd which had gathered, made some taunting remark at her, but Chandri just turned and smiled.

CHAPTER FOURTEEN

THE prison to which the little group was taken was a queer looking building built on the side of a hill, surrounded by a high wall on which a sentry walked. When Dhanraj and Lal went to visit them they found the Christians in good heart, and they were allowed to speak to them through the iron barred gate. Man Bahadur and Bhimsen were on one side of the jail and Sheti, Chandri, Putali and the baby on the other side, but with only a wall dividing the male from the female side. The men were in a room with ten others, and the women with five. They asked Dhanraj if he could get them any blankets as the prison seemed to be cold and damp. He enquired if they were allowed to receive food from outside, and was told yes, but it would have to be inspected by the guards before being passed in to the prisoners.

Before leaving to go back to Baltichaur, Dhanraj and Lal tried to speak words of comfort and encouragement to them.

The next day Jyote and Sister Molly arrived with blankets and food for them all. These were carefully scrutinized by the guards, but the prisoners were allowed to have them.

A week later Lal arrived at the jail and told the prisoners that the police had come for Pastor Dhanraj and he was up before the court now. They gathered at the bars and Lal prayed for him.

About an hour later they saw Pastor Dhanraj coming down to the prison between two police guards.

Man Bahadur and Bhimsen went out to greet him as he came into the prison and he was put in the same room with them. They asked him about his trial and his sentence. He told them how he had been cross questioned on his own beliefs and was asked if he had baptised others. It was suggested he should say that was a Hindu and deny his faith. As, however, he could not do this, he had been sentenced to six years in jail.

They gathered together that evening, in the jail and sang the hymns that they remembered and Dhanraj read out of his Bible which he had been allowed to keep, although the others had been deprived of theirs. The other prisoners in the room crowded round to listen. Some gave abuse but on the whole they sat quiet.

The folks from Baltichaur had been visiting regularly, bringing food and other things they needed. It was hardest for Dhanraj's wife who had to face the possibility of being separated from her husband for six years.

The men and women encouraged each other in the Lord but conditions in the jail were very hard, and there was much quarrelling and fighting among the prisoners.

One day, when Dhanraj tried to prevent a fierce fight, he himself got a badly cut arm. When the folks from the hospital saw it they were very worried about it, and asked permission to bring down some medication for it, but this was refused.

After a month, the time for Maya to report at court again came round. She had visited the group in jail, coming very shamefacedly and telling them how in a dream she had been walking over a field when a large bull came rushing after her. She had started to run away from it, but just when she realised the bull was overtaking her, a white horse appeared and she jumped on his back and was able to escape the bull. This to her was a picture of Christ rescuing her from the power of the devil. She realised that she had denied Him, but that now He had forgiven her.

Jyote told Sheti of a very moving scene in her house where Maya had confessed her sin and poured out her heart to the

Lord in prayer. Maya was quite determined now, she said, to say that she was a Christian, and join them in the jail.

When the folks in prison knew she was going before the magistrate, they all prayed for her, and when later they saw her coming down the side of the hill to the jail, they all came out to welcome her. Then they noticed that she was alone, no guards with her.

"What has happened Maya?" they cried through the bars.

"The magistrate won't let me join you," Maya wailed. "He says I am to go home and report again to him in three months. I told him I am a Christian and have been baptised, but it was no use he wouldn't put me in jail! So I will have to go home."

The prisoners comforted Maya and she left to go back to Chisopani.

It was the rainy season and one night after a particularly heavy fall of rain, the jail was flooded. The women managed to gather their things together and move them to a dry place, but the men's quarters were innundated by the flood. Man Bahadur suffered most as he had tubercolosis. His medical condition had greatly improved with treatment and Dr. Finley had got permission from the prison governor for him to continue having medicine while he was in jail.

Bhimsen, one day, seeing a guard badly treating another prisoner, could stand it no longer and went to intervene. When the folks from the hospital came down to the jail that day what should they see but Bhimsen being publically whipped outside the jail. He put on a brave face but was obviously very much shaken by it.

The guards pressed him to deny his faith in Christ. They argued with him and brought him a paper to sign in which he was to say he was a Hindu and not a Christian. Bhimsen was on the point of signing when he realised it would mean leaving Putali with the baby in jail. So he asked the guards to call Putali. She came out carrying the baby, and wept when she saw Bhimsen's condition. He told her what the papers in his hand said, and added he had endured enough and was going to sign them. He wanted her, since she could not write, to put her thumb mark on them.

The guards spoke persuasively and said that if they signed they would be free and able to go back to their house in a day or two. Putali looked at Bhimsen with his raw bleeding back, and Bhimsen looked at Putali standing holding the baby and looking so thin and wan. He took the pen and signed the papers, and the guard helped Putali to put her thumb print on them.

The jail doors opened and they went back inside. "Only a day or two more now and you will be free," said the guard as he shut the gate.

It was a sad group on either side of the prison that night when the others heard that Bhimsen and Putali had denied their faith. They themselves were miserable when they realised what they had done, how they had let down their friends, and worst of all, Christ Himself.

Dhanraj was particularly depressed and morose the next day when Bishnu Ratna, Man Bahadur's enemy turned up. He had obviously heard from the guards of the signing of the denial and came and spoke sneeringly to him. It was clear that he was delighted and hoped it would not be long before Man Bahadur and Chandri did the same.

Bhimsen and Putali inwardly felt absolutely wretched. They daily hoped for their release, but the days lengthened into weeks and no news came.

Dhanraj and his friends found as time went on they had many opportunities for talks with fellow prisoners, who came from all over Nepal and were in jail for many different reasons. It seemed to them, sometimes, that those who were in prison were the ones who had not been able to pay bribes, not necessarily the guilty ones.

They were able to lend the Bible to some who through reading it became interested in Christianity. The Christian prisoners suddenly realised that here in jail they had ambassadors for every part of Nepal if they became Christians. When released they would go home to places that might never be reached by the gospel had they not heard in prison!

As the months went by and there was still no sign of their being freed, Bhimsen and Putali came into the fellowship again and back to Christ. Dr. Finley, Sister Molly, Jyote, Lal and others from the hospital visited them regularly. All had been saddened to hear of Bhimsen's and Putali's denial. Expecting the two to be released soon, they feared the episode would be hailed as a triumph for the Hindu religion. But when this did not happen and the group were reunited there was great joy amongst the Christian community. There had been much prayer for them all and the promise given by God at this time was: 'Not one of them should break rank.' Through the days and months that followed, this promise held true. Many were the trials and persecutions, gibes and taunts that had to be endured day by day. All had their periods of depression and despair.

It was particularly hard for the women as only Sheti was able to read. For a time they were without a Bible but eventually Jyote managed to get one in to them. Jyote came as often as she could to encourage them, and bring food.

As the time for their release drew near, the Christians at Baltichaur went to the magistrate about this. He said they would only be set free if they agreed to go back to the Hindu faith. Eventually in answer to prayer they were released just before the full year was up, but there was still pressure that they should return to the religion of their forefathers.

A typical hillside village

CHAPTER FIFTEEN

ON their release, Man Bahadur, Chandri, Bhimsen, Putali and Sheti all went to Baltichaur, where the Christians had a feast to celebrate their return. Then they all met round the Lord's table. Maya and Santa Kumari came in from Chisopani for the celebrations.

Dhanraj's wife was wonderful and encouraged the others to witness now they were outside the prison. Everyone wanted to hear of their experiences of Christ while they were put away. Each had their own tale of God speaking to them and undertaking for them in the situations in which they found themselves. Putali told how she had been worried about the baby being ill in the jail and how wonderfully God had protected him so that people now said he looked better than he did before the imprisonment! Man Bahadur spoke of his consciousness of God strengthening him in his body. Bhimsen told of God's help in keeping his temper with the other prisoners.

It was a happy crowd that went back to Chisopani the next day. It had been hard for Maya, Santa Kumari, Juthe, Man Bahadur's brother and the children to keep the farms going, though Lal and folks from the hospital had gone out to help them at the busy time. It was not long before they were all back into the routine rounds of looking after the land and stock, drawing water and all the other duties. Dr. Finley examined them before they went home, and he was amazed how well Man Bahadur and Sheti had kept; truly God's hand had been upon them.

It was about two months after they had come out of prison that Lal came to see his grandfather and came up also to see Santa Kumari and Sheti. He seemed much more diffident and shy than usual and Santa Kumari could not think what was the matter with him. It was not until she was preparing the curry over the wood fire for lunch, and Sheti had gone for water, that he came in and started talking about Sheti, that Santa Kumari realised that he was asking if he might marry her daughter!

"My grandfather is quite willing," Lal said.

"Well then so am I," said Santa Kumari.

Sheti was quite overwhelmed when she came back from collecting the water to receive a proposal, but she shyly accepted him!

It was agreed that there should be a short engagement and that Lal should go ahead and make arrangements for the wedding to be in Baltichaur.

"I would really have liked Dhanraj to marry us and I wondered about waiting until he is released from jail but now I have finished by training I just felt I cannot delay any longer," said Lal.

There was great excitement when the news reached Baltichaur and preparations started immediately for the first-ever Christian wedding to be celebrated there.

It was agreed that there should be an open invitation to all to attend the wedding service as it was a wonderful opportunity for witness. The feast afterwards, however, was to be by invitation only.

When the great day came, Sheti looked very lovely in her white sari, with a white gardenia in her hair. Lal stood smiling beside her in his new Nepali costume. They made their vows to one another and to God before a large crowd of interested spectators and visitors. Then Pastor Timothy, who was carrying on the work of the Church while Dhanraj was in prison, pronounced them man and wife.

Afterwards all the invited guests went to a feast of rice and goat meat curry specially prepared. There was a lot of singing and everyone was very happy, the only thing that marred the occasion was that Pastor Dhanraj was still in jail. The young couple, however, went down to see him as soon as they could.

Jyote was delighted at the thought of having her friend Sheti living so close to her in Baltichaur bazaar.

A Magar woman with a western child

CHAPTER SIXTEEN

IT was some months after Lal and Sheti's marriage that Bhimsen arrived to ask Sheti to come at once as Santa Kumari was ill.

When she heard how breathless and ill her Mother was, Sheti went to Sister Molly and asked her if she would come to the village with her.

They set off early the next morning with Bhimsen and arrived in the late evening at the village.

Santa Kumari was lying on the rice straw mat beside the fire, she was breathing heavily and was obviously very ill. Sister Molly had brought some medicine with her, and this she gave to the sick woman. Santa Kumari smiled and took it gratefully, but she was too ill to talk much, and they were all tired and so were glad to sleep.

The next day Santa Kumari was a little better and able to talk. She said how she felt she was going to die and wanted before she did so to be baptised so that her burial could be as a Christian. Sister Molly had to return to Baltichaur the next day so she promised to get Pastor Timothy to come out as soon as possible to baptize her.

Bhimsen and Putali were there and Maya came over and so they were able to have times of prayer and Bible reading together. The old lady seemed to drink in the words and in spite of being not at all well, was very happy. In the evening as they gathered round the fire for prayer, Santa Kumari began to talk. Sister Molly wondered if she should let her, but decided that it was better for her to do so. Very quietly she told of her life-time fear of evil spirits, and the feeling of walking in darkness, and yet believing somehow that there must be something else. She told of first hearing of Jesus and realising that He was the One true God. Then came the great battle as she faced His claims on her life and what it would mean if she followed Him. How she had failed, and yet she knew now that He had accepted and forgiven her and that when she died she would be with Jesus. She wanted, however, to be baptised so that she need not have a Hindu burial, and to be a witness to all that she had died as a Christian. She herself, however, knew that whether or not she was baptised, it would not affect her going to heaven.

They sang a hymn softly and turned in to sleep. It was about 3 a.m. when Sister Molly felt a gentle shake on her shoulder, and looking up she saw Sheti standing over her.

"Do come at once," Sheti said, "it's Mother. She is making such a strange noise."

Molly rose quickly and went to the old lady, but even as she did so she saw Santa Kumari turn her head. She appeared to smile, but then all was still. Sheti lit a lamp and Molly said: "She has gone, Sheti, you had better wake Bhimsen and Putali."

It was not long before they were all up and discussing plans as to what they should do. They wondered if they could carry the body to Baltichaur, so that she could be buried there. Bhimsen realised he could not carry her alone and Man Bahadur was not strong enough. Others in the village were bound to come to know and how would it be possible for them to have a Christian funeral for Santa Kumari? As Molly was going back to Baltichaur anyway it was decided she should go as soon as possible and send Lal back. In the meantime Juthe and Man Bahadur were to make preparations for her to be buried as a Christian and Lal should take a short service when he arrived.

When dawn broke, Sister Molly left and the others prepared the body. It was not long, however, before the Mukhia and members of the village council came and asked what they were doing. Bhimsen tried to avoid replying, but Mukhia said, "You are not to bury her as a Christian." Bhimsen retorted: "That was her dying wish."

"But she was not baptised was she?" the Mukhia replied, "therefore, she is a Hindu and must be cremated as such. You are not to touch her; she is still a Hindu."

Bhimsen and Man Bahadur argued with them all day over the body. At last it was agreed that Bhimsen and Juthe with two others from the village should carry the body and it should be cremated. The Christians decided that they would have a memorial service among themselves when Lal arrived.

It was a sad party that went down the hillside with the body of Santa Kumari. Bhimsen and Man Bahadur, remembering the old lady's wish, were grieved that they had not been able to fulfil it. They were happy, however, that she had died believing and that she was now in the presence of the One she had come to love in her old age.

It was early the next morning when Lal arrived having hurried as quickly as he could after he got the news. He walked through most of the night, and it was a very disconsolate group that he found awaiting him. After Sheti had got him a rice meal, and he had slept, they all gathered together for a service of prayer and remembrance. It was a very simple little gathering when they all sat round on the straw mats on the mud floor of the room that had been the kitchen and living room and where Santa Kumari used to sleep. Bhimsen and Putali now slept in an attic room reached by going up a pole on which steps had been chipped out and which was propped upright on the floor to an opening into the attic room above.

Now that Santa Kumari was dead Bhimsen and Putali would have to run the small farm on their own, just as she had done when they were in prison. They would grow maize, millet and wheat and they had three or four goats, a few chickens and a buffalo for their milk supply.

Bhimsen told Lal how several people had expressed an interest in Christianity in the village since he came out of jail. "I feel I know so little and wish you were here, Lal, so that you could talk to them. It would make such a difference to us, too, if you were here. We would have Sunday services and you could teach us."

Lal looked at him. "Would you really like that?" he asked. "You know God has been speaking to me about coming back here to live. I have finished my training and if Sheti and I moved out here we could perhaps be of some help medically to the district. The hospital would let me have medicines. Also my grandfather has offered me a piece of his land to farm for him. I have been wondering about it. If I am here I could help you with your sowing and ploughing and we could also help Man Bahadur, for as you know, now we are Christians the Hindus won't and we will need to stand together." together."

"We have been praying, Man Bahadur, Chandri, Putali, Maya and myself," Bhimsen said, "that you might feel that God was calling you to come back here to live, Lal. We could talk to Pastor Dhanraj and Timothy about the possibility of you being set aside as our leader and pastor. We believe God has great plans for this district.

"Yes God has certainly done great things for us, and He will do even greater in the future, I believe," said Lal, "for who is so great a God as our God?"